MW00643887

Sesquicentennial Edition

Celebrating 150 years of Catlettsburg's History

numbered and limited to
nine hundred and fifty copies signed by the author

No. _603_

This book is presented to

Teresa Harmon

with best wishes from the author

Billy C. Clark   7/13/99

Sept. 1, 2000

Billy C. Clark

To Leave My Heart at Catlettsburg

Introduction by
Edwina Pendarvis

Jesse Stuart Foundation
Ashland, Kentucky
1999

Dedication

To my wife Ruth. To Jean Marie and Earl Lockwood, Tina
Dean, and Jim Gifford. To my son Billy and daughter Melissa.
To the grandchildren Benjamin, Timothy, and Jodie. And
to my sister Mary Frances. These poems for your keep.

Billy C. Clark
To Leave My Heart at Catlettsburg

Copyright © 1999 by Billy C. Clark

FIRST EDITION

Library of Congress Cataloging-in-Publication Data

Clark, Billy C. (Billy Curtis)
    To leave my heart at Catlettsburg / Billy C. Clark ; introduction
by Edwina Pendarvis.
    p.   cm.
    ISBN 0-945084-75-7
    1. Mountain life--Appalachian Region--Southern Poetry.
2. Mountain life--Kentucky--Catlettsburg Poetry. I. Title.
PS3505.L2425T65   1999
811' .54--dc21   99-23489
                                                                              CIP

Book Design by Brett Nance

Published By:
The Jesse Stuart Foundation
P.O. Box 391 Ashland, KY 41114
(606) 329-5232 or 5233

Contents

Introduction

If I could give to you it would not be
Of monetary worth as values go,
Rather, a gift of saved up memories
Found along a creek so long ago.

These lines from Billy C. Clark's poem "The Gift of Catlettscreek" make a fitting introduction to this first collection of his poems. They summarize modestly and simply what this book offers his many readers: a gift of memories gathered along the rivers and creeks near the town of Catlettsburg, the river town he has made famous through his prose works. Billy Clark has fashioned poetry that brings special meaning to Kentuckians and great pleasure to readers everywhere. His poems delineate a unique geography, a unique people, and a unique wisdom gleaned from his intimate association with Appalachia's river culture.

Born in 1928 in the small town of Catlettsburg in eastern Kentucky, Billy Clark grew up where the river forms the boundary of three states: Kentucky, West Virginia, and Ohio. His father Mason, one of the great old-time fiddle players, made a living as a cobbler. His mother, Bertha, took in laundry and raised nine children, helping them to stay optimistic and open to life despite economic hardships.

Providing a nice complement to the agrarian poems of Jesse Stuart and many other Appalachian poets, Clark's poems describe not a farming life deeply rooted in the soil but the musical ebb and flow of life in the river town of Catlettsburg at the confluence of the Big Sandy and the Ohio:

The big Ohio blue, the Big Sandy green
Downstream for at least another mile or two
Two colored ribbons waving side by side,
Mixing in heavy rains and swollen tide.

These two rivers were crucial to Clark. They offered him pleasure, adventure, and a means of livelihood as a boy and a young man. His poems tell of trotlines baited with doughballs boiled in water and scented with anise to catch channel catfish at the mouth of Catlettscreek and in the big rivers. They tell of trapping mink and muskrat that came down to the river's edge. Through these efforts, he helped his family by adding to their meager living.

The poems in this book invite readers back in time to walk along the banks of younger rivers, to "leave awhile a world of strife/For boat, trotline, and barlow knife." Clark's many river poems express his pleasure in hearing the river's song and in watching its creatures, from the majestic Great Blue Heron to the humble muskrat. His poetry brings back the old paddleboats that used to traverse the river and recalls the showboat with its brass calliope and churning paddlewheel. He relives childhood adventures on and in the river.

In "First Rollers," he and other local boys swim out into the river to meet the waves made by the paddlewheeler's big wooden blades. In this dangerous game, the boys swam toward the boat until they could feel the push of the rolling waves. Then they let the water carry them back "bobbing in roller waves that washed us home." Another poem tells of his first attempt to swim the breadth of both rivers, the Big Sandy and the Ohio. In the cold wintertime, when swimming was impossible, he continued to play on the rivers and creeks. In "Skating on Catlettscreek, " he tells about wearing home-made skates with blades carved of dogwood and laced with rawhide leather. He tested the thickness of the ice, he says, and when it would bear his weight, skated along on the frozen surface of Catlettscreek. There in the midst of winter's silence, he enjoyed the graceful beauty of the frozen willow limbs, which bent "tip-penciling on lean tablets of powdered snow,/ designs quickstolen by a sweeping wind."

Clark devotes a sequence of four poems to a place of which he is especially fond, the West Virginia Point, which juts out into the river, "hemmed by a different state on either side…a hallowed Point that knew two river tides." From this point he watched the moving surface of the river and the still shape of a nearby sandbar as he listened to calls of the killdeer. In the second of these poems, he tells about the sandbar in early morning light, the "tracktales" of turtles, musk-rats, mink, and raccoon. Having spent so much of his early life out-doors, Clark learned to look deeply into nature to read her stories. He grew to regard nature as his teacher, his playful companion, and a munificent guide. He describes the whitebarked sycamore as making a puppet show for him "with spreading limbs and reddish balls/ On puppet strings like dancing dolls." A moonbeam path shows him the way home, "Between illuminated maple trees that show/my way downriver as I homeward row." This close company with nature developed Clark's sensibility.

Windmade marks left by water rippling against the sand, willow leaf traces in the snow, animal tracks in the dirt, these and other natural signs gave Clark his love of writing, of leaving a memory trace for others to read and follow. He says in the poem "Run Me A River" that, as a child, he scribbled dreams in the sand with a willow stick. These dreams must have been his first poems.

Clark learned not just from nature but from friends and family, too. In a way, these poems are like the wreaths in his poem "Decoration Day on the River." Like wreaths thrown on the river for people who have drowned, these poems commemorate some of the many people who were important to his life. Through dedications to boyhood friends such as Earl Lockwood and Sid Rice and to his friend Alfonso Lombana, as well as through entire poems, Clark pays literary tribute to citizens of Catlettsburg and its environs.

"Shantyboat Man," describes Saul Patton, who was born on a shantyboat and lived on that same boat for eighty years, watching the river from a rocking chair on its deck. According to Clark's poem, the river was the only book Saul Patton ever read, but Patton shared with the young Clark his knowledge about how to make a willow chair, how to set a trotline, and how to weave a net. In this poem, the author shows that although the shantyboat man was illiterate, he was also a learned man in important ways.

Clark writes about "Aunt Lottie" a fictional character based on a real life uncle with whom many readers became acquainted in Clark's autobiography, *A Long Row to Hoe*. "The Death of Aunt Lottie," the longest poem in the book and perhaps the most touching, tells the story of an elderly aunt who is blind and who leaves her treasured dulcimer to her young nephew.

Clark's immediate family, his mother, father, and his wife are honored in several of his poems. His mother and her fondness for having her fortune told by gypsies are subjects of his poetry as is her annual reading of tombstones on Decoration Day. In a stanza in "The Death of Aunt Lottie" he speaks of his mother remembering the dead: "And always Mother with hands on her hips/ Reciting again the name, the year, the day." He writes about his father humorously, with his father gently reprimanding him for not devoting enough literary space to his fiddleplaying. "How simple would have been the chore/to have told about his fiddle more." He reaches back a generation to write a ballad about his Grandpa Clark, a coal miner.

Memories and tributes are important to everyone who feels sharply the transience of things and people they love. This collection of poetry expresses the author's awareness of past and future losses. In "My Vigil Keep" he writes that a floodwall now entombs the river spring "where once I knelt tempering the heat of day." He writes about the disappearance of some of the valuable diversity in nature. Because their homes are destroyed, he says, some songbirds are no longer heard along the river.

In "The Mussel Bed " he looks back to an older time and older losses. On the West Virginia side, once could be found mussels in abundance, such a large bed of them, he writes, that Shawnee camped there "gathering by day, eating under moonlit sky." Sensitive to problems caused by industrial pollution and poor husbandry of the river, he writes regretfully of changes. "I came upon your shore to grieve" he says as he watches the river die slowly "man-plagued." Clark does not rebuke others for these changes without admitting his share of the guilt: "By standing silent I cannot in ignorance claim/To remain uncounted from those who share the blame."

His years of experience on and near the waterways of eastern Kentucky gave Clark a unique wisdom. In "Legend of the Writing Spider," he writes of folklore surrounding the writing spider, more commonly known as the corn spider. According to Clark, popular legend has it that if the writing spider hears your name and writes it across his web, you will die before the sun goes down. In this poem, the speaker addresses the spider, accusing it of plotting to find out the names of passersby so it can destroy them:

> *Your place to plot at night*
> *To coax the name from who day-pass*
> *Your pencil-legs to write*
> *In zigzag strands of wider stroke*
> *The name of whom you found*

Folklore, mythology, even fairy tales, such as "Rumpelstiltskin," contain many references to the power gained over someone when their name is known. These legends may now seem foolish, but they are rooted in universal truths. The tales probably grew out of biblical and other strictures against pride. Modesty and humbleness are considered virtures in most religions, and to seek fame is regarded as a sign of pride, which "goeth before a fall." Clark expands this idea in "The Virgin White Oak," which asserts that this valuable oak tree is jeopardized as soon as its existence becomes known to others. Only in having others unaware of it is it safe from harm: "its life is best assured unknown, unseen."

Clark's lessons are learned from the skies as well as the earth and water. What he learned from the shooting star can benefit us all: "To know the star that burned the sky/held magic not in where it flew/but only on the journey to." It is not mortal life's end that is important, this poem says, but how we live our life. In another poem, "Don't Grieve for Me," he reassures his wife Ruth, telling her that if he dies before her, "I'll throw you down a shooting star/some night to show the path we go." This poem recognizes that the lives of those who precede us can guide us in living our own lives. Everyone has the potential to be a model.

In common with his fellow poets Jesse Stuart and James Still, and perhaps with most Appalachians, is Clark's belief in democracy and equality. Maybe this belief comes from intimate acquaintance with hard labor and the dignity such labor gives to those who endure it. Clark symbolizes nature's egalitarianism with his poem entitled "The Why and Where of Chicory." The little blue flower is extolled in the poem for its bestowal of grace on the most humble places, even across the scars humans have gouged into the land.

One of the most somber lessons of nature is its reminder of human mortality. All poets have repeated this lesson; and in "Heritage of Corn," Clark renews this oldest of messages. But he also expresses his acceptance of death in this and other poems. In "Epitaph," in which the narrator of the poem speaks from the grave, the narrator says that he is now "cocooned forever in the land of my birth."

A line from another poem offers consolation to death's inevitability. In "Passing Through," the narrator speaks nostalgically of visiting a rough, uncultivated field he loves. It is a field that has known no plow or scythe because it is too rocky. The narrator expresses his great pleasure in this untouched field, wild with windshaken oaks;

and though he cannot stay, his melancholy is mixed with joy: "I cross the field grateful for passing through."

This sense of appreciation for earth and its creatures runs through all of the poems in *To Leave My Heart at Catlettsburg* and results in a poignant literary tribute, a gift to a town and its people. Beyond that, this book reminds all readers to observe the world more carefully and to listen more sensitively, to be more alive to the beauty and struggles around us, to be more grateful for passing through.

Edwina Pendarvis
Marshall University

Edwina Pendarvis, educator and author, was born in Floyd County, Kentucky. She earned a doctorate at the University of Kentucky and currently lives in Huntington, West Virginia, where she teaches at Marshall University. Co-author of three books on education, most recently, *Out of Our Minds*, a study of anti-intellectualism in American schools, she has also published articles on Appalachian culture and literature, including an introduction to the early poems of Jesse Stuart in The Jesse Stuart Foundation's 1998 edition of *Harvest of Youth*. Her poetry collection, *Joy Ride*, is published in a three-collection volume, *Human Landscapes*, by Bottom Dog Press.

Two Boys' Way

To Earl F. Lockwood, my brother
by mutual adoption so many years ago

Grant that we might walk once more
Two boys' way Big Sandy's shore;
To choose a time in early May
When river winds are up and play
In willow trees whose cotton blooms
Are wind-danced to a watery loom
And tatted by the minnows chase
In delicate patterns of downy lace.

To hear once more the catbirds quarrel
Warnings that we come to spoil
Down path of sand and bugle weed;
And yet grey-slated bird you need
Not fear our coming for we come
To hear the haunting chant of drum,
To watch the skipjacks surface breaks
And hear snagsongs the current makes.

To sit with willow poles in hand,
Toe-scratching dreams in sun-warmed sand,
Waiting for evening shadow time
To mock the bullfrogs' driftwood rhymes;
And watch the moon come up to tease
The restless water maple leaves
That curl and catch moonbeams at night
And fire the banks in silver light.

Stay to watch the rising fog
Make ghosts of bar and drifting log,
And from the slough hear once again
A raincrow's call of distant rain;
To leave awhile a world of strife
For boat, trotline, and barlow knife:
Another time, another day,
A river and two boys' way.

To Ruth

Time shall not steal from me this love that's kept
Within my soul where dwells eternal spring,
Unravished by a world that's winter-swept
Love grows more beautiful than rhymes I sing.
Time shall not steal from me the haunting stare
Of eyes that coaxed uncertain lips to say
Of love. And yet I caught love there
To keep if you should ever go away;
Thinking if memory should not suffice
And all my world grew bleak and winter-thin
Within my soul I'd kiss you once, then twice
And ever silent leave you there again.
Where love will keep and shall forever be
Unchanged and kept throughout eternity.

Spiders' Way

They did not see me yet I know
They pitched tents in the field below
My window and I saw them there
Wind-dancing in the morning air.

A spiders' camp beaded with dew
Framed within my window's view,
White tents like puffs of summer clouds
Spider-spun into silken shrouds.

Then under camouflage of sun
They struck their tents their campaign done,
Bivouac complete by early dawn
They left as silent as a yawn.

To leave so inconspicuously
Is how the going ought to be,
The why and where no one to say—
Silent as the spiders' way.

Elegy in a Mountain Graveyard

Come walk along this bony ridge with me
Out to the point where sleeps our kith and kin
Inside a fence of rock and age-old trees;
Walk through the fallen gate that lets us in.
Come sit with me and watch the lizards play
On chiseled stones once carved by untrained hand,
Names and dates that time has stolen away
With wind and rain here in this lonesome land.
And who will say beneath the mounds who lies
Asleep, or know the love they knew,
Erased and left in time to strangers' eyes
Now silent as an early morning dew.
And who will know that once upon a day
We came to share their love but did not stay.

To a Scarecrow

Strawheaded guardian of the autumn corn,
Silent sentinel of hillside farm,
Standing in age-old custom where winds mourn
Through tattered cloth covering your slab-oak arms,
I do not think your job a lonely one
With wooden leg man-planted in the clay,
You the receiver of wind, rain, and sun,
Companion to brown-rustling corn that plays
A summer-mellowing song. I do not think
Man did you wrong shaping your destiny
A wooden specter who at night can drink
Moonwine aged through limbs of black oak tree.
I envy you, Scarecrow, your handsome pay
Of immortality for scaring crows away.

Night of the Singing Hounds

From high the ridge the hunters stop to play
Cow-horn music to low-singing hounds,
Foxfires ash-covered as the hound of day
Slow-trails the rugged land mouthing no sound.
The song of horn houndtalks an ended night,
Ritual-song of fox, hound, horn, and men;
Frost-spun the scent of fox is cocoon-tight
To frozen earth that hounds no longer wind.
From high the ridge sore-footed walkers lag
Their masters down a narrow cow-made trail,
Mute to all boastful talk and hounddog brag
Of bugled voices now on mountain stale.
Night-singing hounds sight-trailing homeward men,
Dreaming of cracklin-mush and burlap den.

Creeping from Winter

Summer is gone and I along this clay
Path pause to watch the hills in winter's mood,
Wind-stripped the naked trees have shook away
My season and now doze in solitude.
Low on the slopes redbud and dogwood bend
From winter's touch, the trailing arbutus
And creeping phlox have sneaked to earthen dens
Leaving their wrinkled trails on frozen crust.
The hills are silent now, and like grey eyes
The mountain rocks are free from summer's green,
Exposed to brightness of a cloudless sky
They blink their freedom from the deep ravine.
I pause to watch, dreaming the while to creep
Away with summer, and from winter sleep.

Heritage

I have given now a heritage to you,
In selfsame land under the selfsame sky,
From here the world is yours alone to do
As it was mine an older day when I
Was passed a heritage my father chose;
Know that your world will mine synonymize,
Where in the end still reaped is what one sows,
To know history repeats itself is wise.
The greatest lesson is still the golden rule;
In the end you will be judged by what you gave
Not how many along the way you made a fool,
Less than the truth will not a reputation save.
Know nothing is new in what you do or say
The gift is to do both another way.

Something There is About a Beech

Something there is about a beech
That grows so deep within a wooded dell
Coaxing those who pass, then to beseech
They write of love with promise of no-tell.

To search for space where those before have told
Love stories left only here to see,
Some of them half a century old
Bark-healed to last sealing their destiny.

Lured by assurance of a secret kept,
Carved in the freedom now of no fear
With pocket knife and hand by love adept
Initials inside a heart, the day, the year.

Intriguing as it is to pass this way,
To read love stories written so innocently,
I wonder if love made the yesterday,
Grew old or slowly died upon the tree.

Where Once a Cabin Stood

While walking out a bluff near home
I came upon foundation stones
Size-matched and placed to form a square,
Signs that a cabin once stood there;
Gooseberries not native to the land
Man-planted now grew out-of-hand
And trumpet vine crept everywhere
Forcing me to walk with care.
I found a chunk of rotting beam
From adze-hewed log to build a dream
End-notched to form a single room
Where love could sprout, then grow, then bloom.
No worry of no neighbors near,
How short each day, each week, each year,
No loneliness in caw of crow
Or mournful songs the winds that blow
Forever in this worrisome land
Against it all their love would stand.
I found a makeshift bench where they
Had sat to rest near end of day;
I saw where once their garden grew,
An old plow point, an old mule shoe.
Then near a dog-rose covered wall
I found a wooden hand-carved doll
Made from the heart of cedar wood
Given with love and hopes it would
Take the loneliness away
From a child left alone to play
Where everyday is yesterday
The sameness in the search then play
With make-believe, imagined names
Of all her friends she dreamed that came.
I stayed until the end of day
Until the shadows came to play
Like dancing snakes through limbs of tree
Here in this land of ever-be.
I left the doll beside the wall

Perchance a lonely child should call
Out on a dark and endless night
To take away her world of fright.
How long the day, the week, the year
Since love and loneliness once lived here.

On Rachel's Death

I went to see him during the heat of day,
But the time would not have mattered anyway,
Heat-wise an evening offered no reprieve
From heat intense enough to wilt the leaves
Of trees. And on an untraveled path
Where grass crept in the heat had shown its wrath
Now audible for those who chose to pass
Crinkling underfoot like stems of glass.
He stood beside the well looking bone-tired
With a bucket and a gourd on which he'd wired
A hook to hang it up beside the well,
If he'd drawn up water yet I couldn't tell.
I had not been here for at least three years or more,
She had been gone for two of those I'm sure,
And at the time I was too far away
To pay respects on this his saddest day.
He smiled and looked at me I must confess
Like I had been away a week at best,
I stood not knowing what to say or do
He said: "I'm on my way to see her, you come too."
He walked around the slope, bucket in hand
Until we reached a rock-walled spot of land,
A dozen graves beneath a burning sun
Barren and forsaken except for one
Covered with grass as fresh and green as spring,
Sprinkled with flowers to form a perfect ring;
Then kneeling where his knees had made a trench
He spread the water over every inch,
Leaning toward the mound age-slow with care
I heard him whisper: "Rachel, Caleb's here."

Where Two Rivers Meet

I love to sit and hear the currents sing
Their riversongs on snags of willow trees
And from the banks warm days of early spring
Hear brush-mellowed frogsong melodies.
To hear the sough of waves, to see their crest
Measured by watermarks upon the sand,
Watch the Great Blue Heron motionless,
Statuesque on stilted legs scanning the land.
To watch the searchlights of the paddleboats
Penciling the shores light silverspun
Searching the river for all things afloat,
Laying a silver path to mark their run.
A timeless river and a time to be,
Land of my birth, land of the Big Sandy.

Night Birds

Night birds outside my window sing
As if it were forever spring
And they had not had time that day
To say all that they had to say.
Of course I only speculate,
Could be they quarrel at one come late
Crowding them upon their perch
Where in the dark they have to search
The boxwood limb in dead of night
Without the benefit of light.
But whatever the reason be
I'm grateful for their company,
My day too short, my night too long,
Made shorter now by their birdsong.

Showboat

It seems like only yesterday
When in my youth I came this way
To sit upon the wave-washed sand
Waiting until around the bend
The showboat appeared.

Foretold by the calliope
I climbed high in a willow tree
Watching the paddle wheel that churned
Backwards so the boat would turn
To tie-up here.

Townspeople came from everywhere
To watch, to dance, to sit in chairs
And welcome those who crossed the plank
To visit on the riverbank
The people near.

They sang and danced without a care
Moonbeams playing in their hair
And unbeknownst by them of me
Some kissed beneath my willow tree
Without fear.

And with the coming of the dawn
The river silent as a yawn
The showboat slowly churned away
With promise of another day
Again this year.

I closed my eyes dreaming I may
Be pilot of the boat that day
High on the bridge in captain's chair
Giving the orders to tie-up here,
The town would cheer.

Hound, Horn and Popping Wood

Grandpa said he heard the hunters blow
Foxhorn music to their running hounds,
And on a ridge night-feathered black as crow
He saw a foxfire, heard wood-popping sounds.
"Scoot near me boy, them dogs hound-talk a chase
That's worth a pretty." Grandma said: "I declare!
Your Grandpa's old, and childish; a disgrace
He'd lie to one so young. Ain't nothing there!"
Grandpa winked—and Grandma didn't see,
He whispered low—and Grandma didn't hear,
"Your Grandma thinks hounds are only good for fleas.
It only takes a want to hear them there."
I pitied Grandma knowing that she could
Not hear with us hound, horn, and popping wood.

First Rollers

At Catlettsburg where two rivers meet,
The Big Sandy and the broader Ohio,
Under the willows waiting on sandstone seats
We watched the paddle wheel pushing its tow,
Then swam to see who would be the first
To take the rollers, dangerously close
Enough for wizened rivermen to curse,
Yet close enough for riverboys to boast.
We fought the current, near enough to feel
Wooden blades that churned white river-foam,
Then slipped away as slick as river eels,
Bobbing in roller waves that washed us home.
We scratched our scores upon a sheet of sand
And waited for the next around the bend.

Riversong

Roll on Big Sandy River, roll on,
Will you carry me away with your song,
When I'm done with this old life
My boat, trotline, and Barlow knife,
Roll on Big Sandy River, roll on.

When I'm gone will you float a wreath for me,
Knitted by the wind a pretty wreath to see,
Will you float a wreath for me made from blooms of
    willow tree
Over my watery grave then float a wreath for me.

On my journey will I easy water find,
Strong the current may I easy water find,
Let me easy water find, hugging shore and willow line,
On my journey let me easy water find.

Will the birds then sing for me around the bend,
As they did when I was once on river land,
Catbird, Thrush, Redbird and Wren sing for me around
    the bend,
Will they sing a farewell song around the bend.

Will you miss me when I'm gone Big Sandy,
Will your mournful riversong forever be,
And will you sing both night and day all the ages I'm away,
Will you miss me when I'm gone Big Sandy.

Then roll on Big Sandy River, roll on,
Will you carry me away with your song,
For I'm done with this old life
My boat, trotline, and Barlow knife,
Roll on Big Sandy River, roll on.

Epitaph

This is hill country of ancestral clay,
Land of the fiddle and the horsetail bow,
Of promenade and mournful winds that play
Home-spun ballads lonesome as cawing crow.
A timeless land where once in youth I turned
To walk limb-shadowed paths along their slopes,
Whispering among oak, beech, and fern
Hill-kept secret dreams of love and hope.
Time-aged and on this ridge where lizards play,
I have returned to these beloved hills, my land,
Forever rooted now to sacred clay
Where kindred souls once chose to make their stand.
Akin to rain and sun, rock, tree, and earth
Cocooned forever in my land of birth

After Cherry Picking

They came to visit me today
All dressed out in fine array
Meeting in my cherry tree
A host of feathered company.

On seeing them in rich attire
Their beauty set my thoughts afire
And not the least I must confess
Was seeing them in formal dress.

Birds dressed out in every hue
Catbirds, Redbirds and Robins, too;
In checkered suit and red top hat
Woodpeckers came to eat and chat.

Mockingbirds in tailored gray
Fussed at an arrogant Blue Jay
Threatening those of smaller kin
Sparrows, Bluebirds, Finch and Wren.

And watching them it seemed to me
There were no birds who could agree,

No single bird who chose to share
A cherry with the others there.

Reminding me of my own greed
Picking cherries beyond my need,
Tired of inching out each limb
Plucking cherries from their stem.

Beneath a hot and blazing sky
Red dots that wouldn't leave my eyes,
I thought to stop and make amends
By leaving some for feathered friends.

But little did I know that they
Would choose to spend the live-long day
Quarreling at what the other ate
Until the day became too late;

Too late to see or quarrel or fight,
Leaving the cherries to the night
And the repertoire of the night-dressed owl—
We all were tired of cherries now.

The Hawk

With talons clenched to bone-white limb
Of cedar stitched to craggy wall
He sits alone on mountain rim
A high-ridge perch of vast see-all;
A vigil point to start his fall
Soundless of flight or victor's call.

Through shadows to valley below
Free-falling blur mottled and gray
To where the fern and lichen grow
Graveyard of a predator's prey
Bare bones left to slow decay
In timeless land of nature's way.

Ballad of Emmalee

Come sit with me tonight my Emmalee,
Come sit with me beneath the Sourwood tree,
And we'll make honey sweet as honeybees,
Come keep the promise that you made to me.

The children are asleep now Emmalee,
Let's keep this night and let tomorrow be,
Not lose the magic that we treasure so,
Found under the Sourwood tree so long ago.

And Emmalee she came while children slept,
Under the Sourwood tree her promise kept,
Staying until the stars faded from sight,
Then left a promise of another night.

Under the Sourwood tree where they were wed,
Under star-beaded sky their promise said,
To speak of love each anniversary,
A promise kept under the Sourwood tree.

Run Me A River

Run me a river made by a mountain spring,
Lace the banks with cotton willow trees,
Bead upon the limbs birds to sing,
Temper it all with a gentle breeze
That's river-cooled; and then from far away
Let me hear a raincrow once again
Singing upriver near the end of day
His haunting melody that begs for rain.
And then on mirrored surface ripple-free
May I see reflections of a time gone by
When through the bugleweed and buckberry
A young boy came under a cloudless sky
And with a willow pencil-stick in hand
Scribbled a dream upon the wave-washed sand.

To Mom and Dad upon Their Courtship

Not far from where their tombstones are
My father came under the stars
To court my mother in secrecy
They never told the reason be.

Only that they met at night
Where their love was lost from sight
Of others; and they whispered so
Their love was only theirs to know.

They stayed until the hour was late
Near the cemetery gate,
Under a soft star-beaded sky
Safe in their place less frequented by.

And now their love forever keeps
Where once they met near where they sleep,
And others will not hear or see
Their love or know the reason be.

Sourwood Hollow

Within my memory the hollow that
Ran deep and dark behind my mountain home
Held oak, beech, and ash of virgin growth,
Sawlogs to test the strongest span of mules
Snaking them down the tramroad long gouged out
And smoothed by men and mules another day.
Here at the hollow's mouth mules stopped to blow,
Catching the always-wind that's hollow-made
By trees on slopes that slow-release the sun
And use the deep ravine to store the shade.
In memory of many years ago
I stood in awe watching sweat-lathered mules
Heaving and twitching, shaking off the flies
To fall like nuts from frost-touched walnut trees.
I heard men scold then fuss and curse with words
To fetch a boy a whipping to repeat:

But repeat I did being taught that hills don't tell,
And being told to teach a mule who's boss,
Curse I did pretending stumps were mules,
Acting the part that comes with being old,
But searched with cautious eyes so none would see
Me whisper to imaginary mules
Words honey-sweet as blooms of Sourwood tree.
The way of men, I'd heard my mother say,
To temper burdens with their pretty words.
The hollow dark and deep was home to me,
Often I came just at the break of day
When night-fog hung from silhouetted trees
Like ghost-wash hung to dry in coming sun,
Drip, drip, dripping from the limbs of trees
Drip-songs played on leaves an autumn's old.
The hollow, ridged by hills on either side
Was never, ever more than tramroad wide,
Sloped up with points as sharp as layoff plow
And high enough to furrow wind-drift clouds.
From high the ridge aged red cedars leaned,
Twisted and gnarled with sapwood turned to grey,
Clinging for life in cracks of sandstone cliffs
With birdclaw roots bone-white with coming death;
Yet roots if whittled with a pocket knife
Still held red heartwood, sapwood stripped away
To hold for eighty years a hillside post
Or make a pretty for a boy to boast
While giving to a girl with bonnet set.
Above it all crows cawed their lonesome songs,
From ridge to ridge the turkey buzzards searched
For death upon this lonesome, timeless land
(Or for a boy who would not mother-mind).
Inside the hollow's mouth on summer nights
I searched to find deserted belly mines
Where ice still hung like grey beards of old men
The last of winter in this land to thaw.
Here stories came to life for I could hear
From deep within the creaking carts of coal
Pulled by bank mules so long in dark now blind,

Mines dark and deep and haunted by the sounds
Of picks striking into the veins of coal
Bleeding black dust on men stretched out below;
Too narrow for a stand, too foul to breathe
Taking in the end their heart and soul.
They carried their education on their backs.
And with imagination mixed with fear
Of ghost or seeing miners who
Were buried in the cave-ins long ago,
The ones mine-widows brought the flowers to
And placed near mouths of caves for all to know
The dream once shared lived within them still;
I thought I saw the blinking miners' lamps,
And smelled the acrid gas of carbide light,
I thought that I could hear my father's voice
Warning me to book-learn hard at school:
A pencil to replace the miner's pick
And educated in the head the rule.
I listened and I heard the mountain say
To gather what I wished to store away,
That nothing was forever, but the best
Keepers of them all were memories made.
Safe-tucked away this one I chose to keep,
The once upon a time the hollow that
Ran dark and deep behind my mountain home.

Betwixt and Between

Most often life is all about
Too little to keep, too much to plow out,
Greater than zero, less than the mean,
Most often a life of betwixt and between.

Ode To A Whippoorwill

I never met as I recall
One who said he ever saw
The mystic bird of deep ravine
Who sings his haunting song unseen:
Whippoorwill, Whippoorwill, Whippoorwill.
But such a beautiful melody
Does not depend it seems to me
On being touched by human sight
To be the song he sings at night
When all his world is shadow-still
And rising mist is sent aloft
As if ravine is burning off.
In splendor of an afterglow
I hear his song too lovely though
to mock, but try I will.
Then answering me by his choice
Aware of imitative voice,
I wonder could the reason be
To share the melody with me
And star-beaded sky above the hill?
A melody so sweet and clear
Only the bird and I can hear
The song that lingers through the dawn
I can't quite put my finger on,
But try I will, I will, I will.

The Coming of Rain

The rain came in upon the trees
Carried by a gentle breeze
And sprayed on me by squirrels' play
Made all the difference in the day

And future days of summer-hot,
Breezeless, trees rain-forgot,
To savor from a memory
Wind, rain and squirrels in a tree.

A Favorite Place

There is a place along this river that
I favored more than all the rest combined,
The mouth of Catlettscreek where once I sat
At an early age casting my fishing line,
Fishing for channel cats that lay in wait
For what the running mountain creek would bring
To eat; and I with willow pole stayed late
Coaxing them to take my bait and sing
My line far out into the larger streams
That met but kept their river colors true,
The big Ohio blue, the Big Sandy green
Downstream for at least another mile or two.
Two colored ribbons waving side by side,
Mixing in heavy rains and swollen tide.

The Journey To

When young I saw a shooting star
And thought I'd follow it how far
I didn't know and didn't care,
Youth seldom ask the why or where.
A shooting star I had heard say
Because of coming Heaven's way
Touched down would hold a pot of gold
Like rainbow legend I'd been told;
And legend of Swift's silver mine
In Appalachian hills to find.
My going would cause no concern
The old warned I must live and learn
Myself until I grew more wise
To know the star that burned the sky
Held magic not in where it flew
But only on the journey to.

Death of a Mountain Fiddler

Aged that night, his back time-bent and slow,
He stretched, lifted his fiddle from the case,
Fondled it, twisted the loose-haired bow,
Rosined the horsehairs at a quicker pace.
From doorsill seat the winter slopes he scanned,
Crowfooted eyes that searched eternal spring,
With fiddle chinned like rock to frozen land
He touched once more his gifted bow to string.
Hoedown age-gone, a ballad now he played,
Bleached boards low-sung the fiddler's pat
Of cadence foot wizened to promenade
Drip, dripping on the wood below where he sat.
He left his music to a mountain wind,
In land where mountain ballads never end.

Heritage of Corn

Walking among long rows of autumn corn,
Slow on this flat as shuffling mountain wind,
With back time-curved matching a hunter's horn
And dry as seasoned oak, I bend
Working this corn, feeling akin to seed
I pushed in spring beneath red mountain loam;
Together we have struggled with the weed,
Blistering sun, stump root and hillside stone.
I walk hair-white matching young tasseled ears
Of corn, while hands now wrinkled as the clay
Feel furrows in this face the bull-tongued years
Have plowed as I this field another day.
Heredity of man to corn is thin:
Seeded in earth he will not sprout again.

Ritual Dance

This is the season of the timber moon,
A night of dance, raft songs of coming day,
Haunting ballads speaking of parting soon,
It is a night young lovers slip away,
Leaving the old to dance upon hard crust,
Wrinkle-faced they share an older dream,
And memories time-learned of love and trust
While poling logs down swollen mountain stream.
Alone they dance and rest until the dawn
Fires the ridge and spreads along the slope,
Young lovers whisper now of quick return,
The old whisper of reassuring hope.
Young lovers dreams are of returning soon,
The old to know another timber moon.

The West Virginia Point (1)

On the West Virginia Point I used to sit
Hemmed by a different state on either side,
Fishing the seam where two great rivers met,
A hallowed Point that knew two river tides.
Kentucky on my left where I was born,
Ohio on my right where often I
Would swim to work in fields of bottom corn,
Log-drifting back under a night-dimmed sky;
Stopping along the Point where moonbeams danced
To undulating sounds played under stars,
Wind-made wave-songs in slow cadence
Leaving their ripple mark along the bar;
Slipping into the river, swimming for home
I left the Point tucked in a riversong.

The West Virginia Point (2)

Off of the Point on the Kentucky side,
A sandbar rose some twenty feet away,
Height and breadth depending on the tide,
But always sand enough for birds to play
And search for worms and snails at water's edge,
The bobbing Killdeer with his song: Kill-dee';
The stilt-legged Heron standing where sand was dredged
By undertow not visible to see.
And on the bar in early morning light,
Unless the waves had come to wash away,
Night-stories told by those who wrote at night,
Track-tales with endings where they slipped away:
Turtles, muskrats, mink, and wily coon
Who chose to leave ahead of a fading moon.

The West Virginia Point (3)

The West Virginia Point once home to me
Split rivers like an upturned lay-off plow
Convexed and edged with willow seedling trees,
And beyond the willows the remains of a scow:
Ribs of an excursion boat that had one night
Misjudged the run of sand and run aground,
Its rotted skeleton now a ghostly sight,
The pilot of the boat was never found.
And it was said on nights when stars were out,
Within the darkness you could see him there,
And hear below the surface sand-gritting sounds
Of keel, then hear the pilot shout.
I searched for sunken treasures but found
Only the ribs with their wave-washing sounds.

The West Virginia Point (4)

On one strong rib I tied my first trotline,
Stretched and made it fifty niblines strong,
Made out of extra heavy staggon twine,
Baited where I thought the bait belonged.
For turtles closer in and catfish out
In water where the channel cut through sand,
Coaxing big cats to choose my trotline route,
Swinging the Point to where Big Sandy ran.
To feel and know the quiver of the trot,
Holding my breath for movement with great care,
Movements different from ones current begot,
Knowledge that only came with living there
Upon the rivers in wind, in rain, in sun
Both day and night with want to be as one.

Don't Grieve for Me

Don't grieve for what you cannot see
I will see you, you won't see me
Sitting on a cloud above
Waiting for my own true love
Who promised when I got this far
She'd come to me upon a star
And we'd go skipping hand in hand
On clouds to our forever land.
If you should wonder just how far
I'll throw you down a shooting star
Some night to show the path we go,
It will not really matter though
We'll have for all eternity
My love for her, her love for me.

My Vigil Keep

The path that led down to the river's shore
Untraveled now grows rank with trumpet vine,
The paddle wheels are gone, searching no more
For easy water hugging willow line;
A floodwall has entombed the river spring
Where once I knelt tempering the heat of day,
Habitat destroyed, birds do not sing
Birdsongs once here and now stolen away;
How once it was so long now in the past,
Yet memories that deem my vigil keep,
Passing on a time and place to last,
A reminiscence worthy enough to reap:
A riverland I knew, for all to know
Forever or as long as rivers flow.

Tale of a Shantyboat Man

Saul Patton was born on a one-room shantyboat,
Birthed upon a bed of willow leaves,
For eighty years his home was kept afloat
Tied-up at the mouth of the Big Sandy.
His furnishings were a woodstove and a bed,
And a rocking chair out on the deck at night,
The river was the only book he read,
No formal schooling, he could not read or write.
His education being the riverland,
He chose to share with those who came to set,
From how to make a willow chair by hand,
Setting a trotline, weaving a fishing net;
Or to listen to the stories that he told,
Timeless and each one a river old.

The Death of Aunt Lottie

Aunt Lottie lived alone in a cabin built
Of hand-hewed logs chinked with rock and clay,
Nearby rock cliffs held two gouged-out caves
Eyelashed with grape and honeysuckle vines
That caught a sometimes-wind that swept the slope
And plucked the vines like strings upon a harp
With sightless fingers making a mournful song
While blue-tailed lizards under a summer sun
Danced along the vines like jeweled tears.
Aunt Lottie was blind but well before we reached
Her yard she would be standing on the porch,
One bony hand holding a corner post,
The other waving toward the sound she heard
Different from a varmint's sound or bird's.
She smiled at us although she could not see,
"Stay with Aunt Lottie," Mother would say to me
On this our yearly trip one could be sure
We'd make always on Decoration Day,
Gathering flowers found along the way
To place upon the graves high on the ridge
Of friends and kin, and also to replace
Stones that had fallen from a rock-wall fence;
Refilling graves settled by rain and snow,
Graves with swelling gone now sunken holes
Like those made from a storm-uprooted tree
With log mule-snaked away for winter wood
Leaving no trace that it was ever there.
Turning blind eyes toward my mother's voice,
Aunt Lottie in her birdsong voice would say:
"Lord, Berthy, why worry on this day
You come here carrying flowers for the dead
And think that I will need some tending-to,
Forgetting all the other days when I
Live on this lonesome mountain all alone.
You go, leave Issac not to stay and watch
Me like a tree-perched old black sentry crow."
Turning her sightless eyes blinded like clouds,
She said: "Don't gather flowers from the yard;

I can tell the seasons from their smell."
I did not mind that I was left behind,
Not gone to chase lizards from headstone rocks
While pretending to be cleaning off the graves,
But reading off the names upon the stones,
Some misspelled, others wind-washed away,
And always Mother with hands on her hips
Reciting again the name, the year, the day;
And since to bury meant so far to climb,
The weather being important at the time,
The struggle up the mountain, rain or snow,
She knew or others once had told her so.
When Lottie was satisfied that all were gone,
Cupping her ears to know their going sure,
Her long, gray hair now folded in her lap,
She breathed in deep and savoring the smell,
Waiting our ritual when I would say:
"What flower-smell does the wind now bring?"
"Honeysuckle!" she said, sweeping her hands
Toward the caves where vines and flowers grew,
While wind-caught hair once cooped upon her lap
Swept and trailed out like thin, gray smoke.
With eyes barely inches from me now,
I stared, remembering what mother had said,
That Lottie had not been blind on her birth,
A disease had slowly stolen sight away
When at about my age she could not see
And had so little time for memories.
"What does the wind bring now?" I asked.
"Roses, the ones that have old-timey smell."
Judging Aunt Lottie to be the smartest of
All my kith and kin, I told her so.
She reared back in her back-worn rocking chair,
Split-bottomed and weaved with hickory sapwood bark
That mother had peeled and laced for her one year:
"Now let me see," she said; "see about that!
What grade you in now?" and with open mouth
Held as if to catch what I would say,
To make sure they were not wind-stolen away.

"I'm in the fourth grade now at school," I said.
Rocking back and forth now in her chair,
With burst of energy which scared me that
The creaking rockers might give way and I
Might never know now what she had to say.
And then as quickly as the start was made
She stopped, placing her hands upon her hips
Like Mother often did to emphasize
Intentions for to get the straight of it.
"You got me beat," she said, now clapping hands;
Not bad, you got me beat by only four."
And then she gave her laughter to the wind
That carried out of hearing. And leaning, she
Whispered as if someone might overhear
To fetch her dulcimer she kept inside
Beside her bed and on a table there
That held her Bible that she could not read
But told me once that all she had to do
Was hold it on her lap, faith would seep through.
Breath-held I waited for her hair to catch
In the dulcimer strings although it never did.
She strummed with turkey quill and said to me:
"Lord, Lordy, Isaac, few will ever know
What company this dulcimer is to me!
Lord-sent to fight this awful loneliness,
Music from the heart runs down the arm,
Drops from the finger tips here on the strings:

> *"Give me the flowers while I live,*
> *Trying to cheer me on,*
> *Useless are flowers that you give*
> *After the soul is gone."*

And while Aunt Lottie softly played this song,
I sneaked into the yard and picked for her
Daisies that I brushed across her hand,
I saw the tears well-up in cloudy eyes,
Surprised, I never thought the blind could cry,
With eyes accustomed to a nothingness.
Then Lottie strummed the dulcimer again,
Felt but could not see the tears that fell

Upon the strings, but wiping, sang to me:
"Sweet bunch of daisies
Picked from the dell,
Whisper you love me
Daisies won't tell."
I loved Aunt Lottie and wanted her to know,
Wanted to hug her neck and tell her so,
But mother had cautioned me saying that
Aunt Lottie resented pity and might mistake
Any show of love as simply being that.
She placed the daisies on her lap and I,
Seeing her quivering lips and wrinkled face,
A sound that gave my love for her away.
She touched then ran her fingers over me
With the softness that she played the dulcimer,
Sensing that I might be holding back a cry,
In quivering voice leaned and said to me:
"I can't see you but I know the music's there.
I can hear it in the pat, pat of your feet.
And it makes me powerful happy knowing that
If all the loneliness I've come to know
In these dark hills should ever come to you
Your music will make it skittish as a crow.
When I am gone the dulcimer is yours."
When seven years of schooling ahead of her,
A neighbor brought word of Aunt Lottie's death.
With heavy rains now among the hills,
Bringing the news had made the going slow.
There, Mother said we'd have to sit the night,
Custom forbid for us to leave alone
A body even with the spirit gone,
A ritual: respect paid to the dead.
I thought that I could hear Aunt Lottie quarrel
At mention that she needed tending to,
I remember once she said when she was gone
She was going to a land where she could see.
A land where loneliness would never be.
We buried her in forever-lonesome land
High on the ridge, home of the sentry crow

That often set on top a lonesome pine.
I thought then of a song Aunt Lottie sang:
> *" 'Neath the pines*
> *'Neath the pines*
> *Where the sun will never shine*
> *Winds whisper and the cold wind blows"*

And as we picked our way back down the ridge,
A loneliness I had not known before
Settled on me as evening shadows fell,
I asked to stop to fetch the dulcimer.
"Hush, Child!" my mother said to me,
"You'll bring an omen on the lot of us.
Taking the plunder of the one who's gone
Before the dirt has settled on the grave!"
But in the days that followed people came
To plunder all Aunt Lottie left behind;
Fearing that, I begged to go to look:
"Hush, Child!" my mother said, scolding me,
"The omen's worse on those who take away
Things not promised them beyond the grave!"
I hoped if right, if should the omen be,
The dulcimer would be silent to the quill,
Its music sealed inside Aunt Lottie's grave
Never to hear again, never to see.
And then one day a neighbor came to bring,
(The neighbor who had told us of her death)
The dulcimer Aunt Lottie left with her,
Whispered to Mother she thought Aunt Lottie knew—
A foretelling that she soon would leave the land.
Taking the dulcimer where none could see,
I opened it and laced between the strings
I found the quill needed to strum and play.
And then beside the dulcimer I found
The daisies that I had once picked and gave
Aunt Lottie to show the love I had for her,
That she had kept to show her love for me,
Sealed so the dryness could not tear apart.
Strumming with quill, the loneliness was gone;
I strummed again and found Aunt Lottie there.

Hill Scenes

I love the rugged beauty of these hills,
Hogback ridge with shagbark hickory trees,
Of unpretentiousness, no-nonsense frills
Where what there is is exactly what you see.
Steep slopes with dogwood, ash, cedar and oak,
Hewed log cabins, yellow Jersey cows
With tell-where bells and wood-forked no-jump yokes
Protecting hillside gardens steep to plow.
Stands of shoepeg corn, scarecrows for crows,
Winter wood cord-stacked in lean-to sheds,
Splitrail fencing trellised with pink dog-rose
Home cemeteries rock-fenced to mark the dead.
Pride of possession, a matched-up span of mules,
Of education, a one-room settlement school.

The Why and Where of Chicory

I doubt that I will ever see
A wildflower as lovely as chicory
That blooms when day has just begun
And closes with the heat of sun;
Softness to match an angel's eyes
And all the blue of summer skies.
And, too, I doubt to ever know
Why it should choose to seed and grow
In man-made wasteland greed begot,
Roadsides, worn paths and vacant lots,
Unless it is in Nature's plan
To heal man's scars upon her land
And to each portion so decree
Beauty distributed equally.

Birthright

Here in this Appalachian land where I
Was born because it was my mother's choice
To bear me underneath Kentucky sky
Where I would have both hill and river voice,
To teach me the beauty of the land,
A heritage that I would come to know,
Valleys and cloud-washed hills where I could stand
And see two rivers meeting far below;
To understand and love the people who
Settled this land keeping the selfsame dream
Of living here and not just passing through,
In birdsong hills and willow beaded streams.
I'm grateful that my mother gave to me
A birthright in the land of Kentucky.

Periwinkle

Deep in my woods the periwinkle grows
To mark a plot where those before chose
A gravesight and planted on that day
Periwinkle to crowd the weeds away;
To spread, to bloom, and in absentee
Of anyone to come again to see
After the graves, to come the end of May
To decorate on Decoration Day.
Without human touch the periwinkle there
Would give to those alone perpetual care.

The Virgin White Oak

There is an oak that grows upon my land,
The only remnant of a virgin stand
Where by perchance visitors that see
Beseech me to seek the registry
To list it there where treasures of the past
Have been permitted by man to live and last,
Not knowing that to make its being known,
The seeds that sprout destruction have been sown,
And the very fact that they have happened-in
Has marked now the beginning of the end;
I don't intend their interest to demean,
But its life is best assured unknown, unseen.

Dreamcatch

If time should catch me far away
From my beloved hills,
Not in the end to stay my stay
And dreams left unfulfilled,
There are two dreams among the ones
I'd hate to leave behind,
One of the dark, one of the sun
I searched but did not find:
The cove the whippoorwill once found
At night his song to sing
Rebirth sun-touched in frozen ground
To sprout each coming spring;
Life pretty as a melody
Made in a mountain land
To last as long as everbe
To live again, again.

Nightshadows

When shadows fall upon this riverland,
Trembled by night-wind through the willow trees,
Falling like dancing snakes on beds of sand,
I come to hear a river soliloquy;
To watch the moonbeams soft and cat-paw quiet
Tiptoeing whitecaps caused by rising wind,
Like fireflies with their intermittent light
Reflecting off the water to no end.
A rising mist creates a ghostly night,
Young willow trees sough from the current-play,
Tops bent in time by wind or boy's right
To ride them down to water where some stay.
With night grown old now on this riverland
I leave with promise to return again.

Tree Horse

There is a place we used to go where we
Often stopped to mount and ride a tree
For reasons unbeknown, shaped like a horse,
No-matter reasons then to us of course,
Young and with no interest to discern
Only to ride a horse our days' concern,
One grazing there in fern and deep in moss,
A curved bark saddle and green head to toss,
And limbs upon its neck to hold as reins
Leafed out to visualize green horse's mane.
There is a place we used to go where we
Once rode a horse in our imaginary.

Passing Through

Often I come to sit here in a place
That rims a field and knows no plow or scythe,
Saved by sandstone rocks too deep to pry,
Nothing there is to show a human trace.

Here on this land wildflowers without flaw
Are nurtured in the shade of man-worthless trees,
Hollow first-log beech are hives for bees,
Wind-shaken oaks will splinter to the saw.

The flowers bloom and die upon this land
Where beauty is the only right to be,
Independent of humans here to judge or see,
Fulfilling their destiny in nature's plan.

Often I stay until the morning dew
Glistens at the touch of coming sun
Then scurries under leaves its purpose done,
I cross the field grateful for passing through.

The Mussel Bed

From the mouth of the Big Sandy going upstream
Around first bend and slightly up ahead,
On the West Virginia side once one could glean
Mussels to eat or bait where once a bed
So large the Shawnees chose to camp and rest,
Gathering by day, eating under moonlit sky,
Heaping their empty shells, keeping the best,
With throw-a-ways in heaps of shoulder high.
The best they kept for jewelry and trade
With Indians in camp or hunting bands,
From mother-of-pearl they too their jewelry made;
The Shawnees took theirs to Scioto land.
Downriver dams flooded what used to be
The mussel beds and shells that one could see.

Two Rivers Wide

At the age of seven I pushed off from the shore,
My dream to make the far Ohio side,
A distance I had never swum before,
An attempt to swim alone two rivers wide.
No one to watch or wait upon the bank,
To say that at my age I should not try,
A journey where I either swam or sank
Alone between two rivers and a sky.
I had sight-measured a thousand times or more,
Counted the strokes it took to get me there,
Swimming now with muscles tired and sore,
I fought to catch a dream and not a scare.
Finally feeling fingers clawing sand,
I pulled myself upon Ohio land.

To Kill a Weed

Millions are spent each year to kill the weed
With sprays too numerous to mention on the shelf,
All sending signals to a substance that
Kicks in to reproduce itself:
A willpower unbeknown to stay alive
Against all odds, the weed will then survive.
But if you should ever want to eradicate
You must begin by speaking of a need,
Simply put, to praise and cultivate,
Spending money to hybridize its seed;
To worry and fret while making sure you're near
To that particular weed you want to hear:
Word chemicals and sprays that let them know
How precious to you it is that they should grow.
Then cantankerous as they are to do you in
No matter what you do or what you say,
Even of all the money you will spend;
To spite, the weed will then wither away.
It is the law of nature that to get
What you want you praise the opposite.

Forever Autumn

Autumn is my season of the year,
A time to pause and quietly meditate,
A spring and summer gone, a winter near
That's cold and symbol-marked by death and fate,
The truth of which I would not choose to know,
Knowledge of season's wake or season's sleep,
A timeless pause between a sun and snow.
Instead, I'd choose autumn to hold and keep,
And if a promise of another day,
I'd take the one tinted with harvest brown,
A tempered wind scented with fresh mowed hay,
Night-frost that melts at daybreak on the ground.
Autumn time could not winter-steal from me,
Forever autumn to be my destiny.

Skating on Catlettscreek

With skates made from the wood of a dogwood tree,
And laced with rawhide strings to hold them tight,
The creek slow mountain-bent and wintery,
Wind at my back to make the going right;
One foot to test the ice, one on the shore
To feel a certainty that holds my weight,
Ahead the spider roots of a sycamore
Sprawled in midstream to negotiate;
Willow limbs frozen with ice now bend
Tip-penciling on lean tablets of powdered snow,
Designs quick-stolen by a sweeping wind
That spins snowcones ahead of where I go
Chasing whirling cones down mountain creek
Until the ice ahead thins out too weak.

The Ballad of Ada Lee

Tell me my sweet Ada Lee
If I love you and you love me
Why can't there a wedding be,
Tell me my sweet Ada Lee.

Such cannot be sweet Henry Brown,
Pa says to search until I've found
One who lives on bottom ground
Not one up and not one down.

You on the hill where nothing grows
But troubles and the thieving crows,
Among the rocks the green briar grows
And love melts down like winter snow.

Me down where the bluebirds sing,
Where land as black as black bird's wing
Will make a crop both fall and spring,
Where I won't want for anything.

Oh pity, pity, Ada Lee
Then will you steal away with me
Over the mountain, across the sea
Where our love will ever be.

Sweet Henry Brown I cannot say
For Pa would surely find a way
To search us out and make you pay
And I'd be left to pine away.

Let's keep the love that we have found—
Our world the fox, their world the hound—
A place that others have not found
Betwixt the hill and bottom ground.

Where the Girls Were

A single light when not by weather doused,
Or by some boy with slingshot and a bet,
Burned above the church door and known as
The Sinners' Light, a beacon coaxing stray
Souls from off the mountains to "get right"
Hopefully this side of Judgment Day.
A call to sinners, backsliders, and to those
Who needed re-affirmed before the burn.
And just below the light a message read
"Sinners Welcome." Meaning sinners of every kind
No matter how low-down, how high the perch,
All were short according to Slaboak Church,
According to Bro. Burdock who had let them in
For ninety years without an aspirin.
Built from slaboak boards with bark long peeled,
And sawrig-edged to make a tighter fit,
Now weathered grey the unseasoned wood
Buckled in time from sun, snows, and rains,
Wailed songs as mournful as a dulcimer string.
Sapwood worm-pocked and in the heat of sun,
Blue-tailed lizards jeweled the boards by day,
Mud-daubers carrying mud up from the creek
Patched knotholes and wide cracks to seal away
In mud pipes the food they caught for another day:
Spiders of every size and every sort—
Ground up would cure the shingles or a wart.
Standing on top the ridge and looking down,
The church looked winter-poor, bow-backed and grey,
Quiet except for gossip and revival days
When from as far away as Blaine they came
To heal the weakness of the human flesh,
Repent and let the devil catch the blame.
They brought their daughters here to do the same.
And in the churchyard where a great oak grew
Limb-hovering the land like a setting hen,
Hatched broods of gossip while the hymns were sung,
Ghost-roots of the great oak tree had sprung

Up mounds of earth like those that housed the dead,
In the shadows hid boys with girls from Blaine
Chancing to cheat the Sinners Light to say—
In whispers, glancing shoulder-back in fear
They'd end up a burning cinder as their pay,
For asking to walk them home the mountain way.
And yet for all our mischief, all their fuss
It was the only sign that ever welcomed us—
We chose to take what wrath we might incur
For worldly ways here where the girls were.

Even the Heavens Weep

Will in the course of time these hills that we
Now know and love be taken from our care,
Timbered and stripped for coal then left to be
Wasteland that coming generations share;
Clear-cut, will hills become a terraced town
Spider-webbed with roads and houses that
Are lost from nature's voice to urban sounds,
And creeks along whose shores where once we sat
Be channeled out of sight, sewered below
A crust of concrete, muted and subdued,
The hills then void of all we've come to know,
Alienable to those we never knew;
Hills left scarred from ridge to valleys deep,
So forsaken even the heavens weep.

On the Naming of the Billy C. Clark Bridge at Catlettsburg, Kentucky

To be so honored in my native land,
People-chosen as a favorite son,
A bridge that bears my name now built to span
The river where my life was first begun
Here in Kentucky in this river town
Seems to me an honor that they gave
For my stories and my poems in which they found
Something worthy enough for them to save.

To Watch a Pond

I watch the heron as he wades
On stilted legs near cattail blades
At edge of pond where cattails grow
Brown velvet heads row on row.

Where turtles weave among the reeds
Their wrinkled heads pushed up for need
To see, to breathe reed-filtered air
While snapping bugs that venture there.

And in the shade upon a log
I see and listen to a frog
Practicing for when the hour is late
His courting song to find a mate.

Upon an upturned mussel shell
The water spider weaves her sail
To catch the wind, to quietly guide
Her journey to the other side.

I watch the beaver bob and swim
Holding in his mouth a limb
To weave and seal dam water so
It will not find a place to go.

I dodge a devil's riding horse—
A dragon fly to you, of course—
Swooping to land, then off again
Like an undecided plane:

Witch doctors to me a younger day
With legend how they searched for prey
To feed a witch, to keep her strong
To snatch up boys who came along.

And tales of brown water snakes
Dropping from trees and in their wake
Waves that would for sure ensnare
The unpermissioned swimming there.

Mud daubers in iridescent blue
Search for mud around the slough
For mud-pipe homes to store away
Spiders on which their eggs to lay.

With minnows nibbling at my toes,
A sky above with Van Gogh crows,
And unimagined birds to sing—
I can not add a single thing!

Only to listen and to see
The beauty and the symmetry
As nature waves her magic wand
So that I may watch a pond.

If I Should Go Before

If I should go before you go
And I could leave behind
What I would want you most to know
And in some solace find,
I loved you more the day I went
Than I did the day before,
Though it's hard to know in days we spent
How I could have loved you more.
Forgive me for the things not said
That I had meant to say,
But silent-kept within my head
For such was not my way.
I tried to show by smile and touch
Sight-ways, a love unheard,
Wishing so very, very much
To catch love in a word.
But on that day that you come to
Forever be with me,
I'll whisper that I love you
For all eternity.

Where Once a Spring

There is no path that leads now to the spring,
Or blue-barked beech to hold the birds to sing
Across the meadow at the edge of woods
Where once to rest from cutting hay I could

Go to softly blow a clearing there
And lift the fallen leaves away with care,
A place where I each day could happen-in
A world of water spiders, thrush, and wren.

A spring so pure, so cold, so sweet to taste,
To use beyond a thirst would be a waste,
To savor here in quiet solitude
And leave without a sign that I intrude.

Near the spring moss and wild ferns grew
In shadows where spiders wove their webs and dew
Pearled the strands for more than half a day
Before the sun broke through to steal away.

There is no path where once I traveled to—
Even the woods beyond has been cut through—
A spring now only memory
That keep alive my world that used to be.

The Breaking of Drought

Not by coincidence
Was the difference,
But remembered plans
To parched lands
that say:

No more than they can bear,
Enough for them to share
Either way.

How Shall I Greet You

How shall I greet you on your day of birth,
Here in this world that man has brought you to,
Where computers often calculate your worth
By who you owe and seldom what you do,
Unless you're one of those almost alone
Like Frost who took the path less traveled by,
Content to have accomplishments on stone,
Your epitaph after the day you die.
And will you choose the unheard melodies
That Keats once searched, ones so unheard-sweet,
The ones that for a lifetime-offer tease,
Or authors that you chose to hear and meet.
Grey's paths of glory led but to the grave,
Judged not by who you were, but what you gave.

Winter Thoughts

If I had promise with the coming spring
The mythical gift of rebirth to begin anew,
This winter's time to ponder on the things
To change with second gift of passing through;
I would not choose to change for sake of change,
May not, in fact, decide a change at all,
For certain not to end or rearrange
The seasons, winter, spring, summer, and fall;
I'd keep unheard, unseen, a neverend,
The search more rewarding than the fact,
Beauty always dependent on depend,
Imagination more valued than exact;
I'd keep rebirth still with each coming day,
Not as a myth a winter's end away.

Once a River

I come today upon your shore to grieve,
A vigil almost too sad to comprehend,
Black coal-washed bands on willows mocking sleeves
Banded by man to mourn the death of kin.
Your surface sparkling iridescent hues
So beautiful and yet so sure of death
To native wildlife and those passing through,
From oil, coal, chemicals your length and breadth.
How could I have watched this river that
I love so much, so much a part of me
Die slowly, silently, man-plagued whereat
A reversal seems an impossibility.
By standing silent I cannot in ignorance claim
To remain uncounted from those who share the blame.

A Christmas Story

To Sid Rice, who walked with me for
a sack of hard candy so many years ago

And it is written in this mountain land
He came as soft as snow on Christmas day
To bring the gift of hope to every man
And woman, and once again to say
A promise made within these rugged hills
So long ago and on this day defined
In truth without embellishments and frills,
So beautiful the littlest child could find;
Of how it was He sent His only Son
To die upon a cross of dogwood tree,
And on this day the beginning was begun
Of a life to last throughout eternity.
Eternal life for those with faith to say
They believe the story told on Christmas day.

The Big Sandy

I love this river especially at night,
With a moon that's bright enough for minnows' play,
The riverland wind-hushed and shadow-quiet,
With peoples' world seeming so far away.
A summer's night when crawfish come to shed
Brown-crusted skins on warm wave-washed sand,
While silently the bullfrogs from daybeds
Breaststroke to drifts for ritualistic stands.
Motionless the Killdeer on her nest,
Ground-scraped and lined with grass, pebbles, and stems,
Listens inside the eggs under her breast
To Killdeer chicks conversing from within.
And I the stranger with want but cannot stay,
Leave brushing from the sand my tracks away.

Retold Memories

It's said you can't go home again but I
Have made a solemn promise that I will
Return to be beneath a mountain sky,
Along the rivers and upon the hills;
To be with those once more whom long ago
I traipsed, hunted and fished at will this land,
To reminisce, our hair now white as snow,
In mountain dialect that we understand;
Embellishments to make each story told
Exciting with a storyteller's care,
If need, to put the truth away on hold,
To give those listening-in their equal share.
The gift to tell now how it used to be,
Stories worthy of retold memories.

Decoration Day

We went each year on Decoration Day,
In Big Sandy country the thirtieth of May
To visit the graves of kin and all of those
Who slept high on the ridge in quiet repose.
To decorate their graves, each one the same,
No matter here in dignity or shame,
And also those who no inscription gave
Their being, only an unmarked grave.
For here among these hills a life begun
Ended in sameness for each and everyone
Awaiting Judgment Day, a finality
Of forever death or life eternally.
For flowers we chose wild daisies and violets,
Dog-rose, fern leaves, all stems kept wet
Bundled in washing tubs and stored away
For the procession on this special day.
Up, up the mountain slope tub rings in hand,
We kept our ritual in this timeless land.

How Much You Mean to Me
(To Ruth)

For me to say how much you mean to me
I'd need to start with words this mountain's high,
In depth more deeper than these rivers be,
Broader than this Appalachian sky;
With all the birdcalls gathered in one song.
And all the seasons ladled into one,
Each word poet-placed where it belongs
That speaks of love greater than that begun;
Beauty beyond the wildflowers that we saw
A day so long ago in wooded dell,
Our love more haunting than a night-wind's call,
Beyond the reach of all my words to tell.
So high, so deep, so wide in beauty wrought,
A love beyond my power to say, word-caught.

To Leave My Heart at Catlettsburg

The snows of winter whisper in the wind
That it is time for my return once more,
With promise that I will not leave again
Among these hills and on this river's shore;
To see and talk with those long left behind,
Though many now are sleeping on the Hill,
To make-believe those things I cannot find,
With waning strength and yet a stronger will.
Land of my stories, poems, so far away
Where stands a bridge Kentucky gave my name,
And from the hills and hollows on that day
The people from this rugged valley came
To speak of love and pray for my return
Among these hallowed hills where I belong,
Expressing hope but also great concern
That I might put it off and wait too long.
They spoke of those who could not write or read
How to them my books were read to show
My love; how they expressed the need
For all the mountain folk to hear and know.
Bestowing the greatest tribute that could be
A writer's; of how they laughed and cried
From stories read and lines of poetry,
Choosing to keep my books at their bedside.
How in the end they whispered soft and low
Their question, hoping that the answer would
Be that on this trip I had not planned to go
Away, but had returned for good.

Queen Anne's Lace

If in a poem I could retrace
The intricacy of Queen Anne's Lace
And find the beauty there within
I'd have myself a poet's pen.

On the Reading of My Book Dedicated to My Father

Having hardly learned to read or write
He asked if they might read that night
A story from my published book
Allowing for an occasional look
At words he could not read to know
Their meaning and yet deemed it so
It took both hearing and a sight
To know if he had raised me right:
To love my people and my land,
That truth came seldom second hand.
Then sending word to me to tell
Though I had written tolerably well
How simple would have been the chore
To have told about his fiddle more.

Winterdread

I am not one of those who winterdreads
Nor sees it symbolic of perpetual sleep;
Instead, I love this season when night spreads
Hoarfrost upon these rugged hills that creep
To jewel the land below a winter sky,
Sparkling in tepid sun and tempered cold,
Night-spun pearls of frost that beautify,
Gathered by a sun a daybreak old.
When cloud-dusted snow as soft as feather-down
Is carried by the whisper of a wind,
Building a Christmas scene upon the ground
More lovely than a mind can comprehend.
Winter is but a pause stop for most things,
Between an autumn and a coming spring.

Winterbirds

I watched the redbirds drop with flakes of snow
Like sunburst through thin clouds of winter so
Devoid of sound it took keen eyes to see
Them slip with snow inside the holly tree
To search through dark green laminated leaves
For berries dropping some as if to please
The quarreling birds under the limbs below
On frozen earth building a winter's snow
Still see-through thin for berries to be found
Under the tree scattered along the ground:
The Titmouse, Finch, Junco and Chickadee
All ruffle-feathered cold and wintery,
Caught in a season of their least content,
Their time of plenty now an autumn's spent,
Time of rebirth long as a winter old,
A land now turning white, wind-swept and cold
With a winter here to stay its stay,
A time to come, a time to go away,
Fulfilling now that part of nature's plan
For winterbirds upon a winterland.

On Building a Dream

Dreams are things by mind or eye
We thought or saw as we passed by
When by our choosing to refrain
Found a niche within our brain
Lying there in dormancy
Filed under immaterially
Unknown until one magic night
Giving the freedom from respite
Chose to reappear once more
With greater importance than before:
A day-sown thought, a night-dream reap,
Haunting and with no choice but keep.

An Appalachian Once

I will not see again within my time,
And such may never, ever be again,
Trees growing too tall for a boy to climb,
A stream still pure enough in which to swim;
To see a meadow stretched upon a loom
Woven with wildflowers in an early spring,
Breathe air scented by the sourwood bloom,
Listen to melodies bird-made to sing;
To hold within my hand loam so complete,
Land that man had not yet laid to waste,
Growing food to share and enough to eat
From heirloom seed time-tested kept for taste.
I will not know again a land so fair,
An Appalachian once, no longer there.

The Walkingstick

Of all the insects I have seen
The Walkingstick remains supreme
By single or by hodgepodge
In oddness or in camouflage,
A foremost antonym of quick
She is more stickish than the stick
Where she leaf-eats and can be found
Dropping her eggs down to the ground
Then paying no attention to
Their survival rate of none-to-few
But to survive's a touch of fame
No other insect can lay claim
In a court of nature's law
Looks unparalleled by all.

Late Autumn

Late autumn is a time I see
Nature's magic symmetry
Of leafless trees, limb-penciled sky
Autumn hues that tease my eyes,
Leaf carpets on a wooded land
Hickory yellow, black oak tan,
Crimson maple, dogwood red
Tufted where the berries bled,
Blues, yellows, reds, and greens
Intermediates in between,
Wildflowers scenting autumn air
Haunted by bees who court them there
And kiss their blooms, steal and leave
Woods-lovers now alone to grieve
In bedded leaves where few will see
A love or beauty used-to-be,
And high above the land and trees
Forming their haunting, timeless V's
Geese-symphonies now fill the air
Coaxing I come, I know not where.

Dream Search

There is a river where so often I
In memory return to be once more
Again to see, to touch, to satisfy
My want of dreams once left along its shore.
Nearby a run of hills where often too
In memory again at eventide
I yearn to feel nightwinds, touch morning dew
Along their wooded slopes where dreams abide.
A Kentucky river-mountain foothill place,
A sliver of land where young dreams once were made,
Indented deep enough to leave their trace,
Nurtured long enough to then have stayed.
A wanderer's dreams kept in memory
Transcending miles and time to know, to see.

Death of a Miner

He crawled into the belly mine before
Daybreak and inched the narrow floor,
By headlamp-light carbide and water fed
Stretching to push his miner's pick ahead

To reach the niche picked out the day before,
His shoulder-waddled bed; with arms still sore
And eyes made red from dust that fell like dew
From seam above he'd picked a long day through.

Aged, he dreamed no more or vowed to find
Daywork outside the lonely mine,
Nor swore to know daylight, the sun, the rain,
No tunnel-grave to crawl inside again.

Like those before, he stayed too long to go
Before the miner's curse crept in his soul
To occupy the end of every dream
To find a longer, richer, thicker seam.

So cold, so dark, so damp, so foul of air,
A misery with nothing to compare,
A lust that lured the only way to go
Down and deep to find the love of coal.

Where down and deep ran out of turning ground,
A place where jilted miners' bones were found
Where lust and lure no longer need enslave—
And love of coal was in the end his grave.

To Quote a Poem

Be there a poet who ever wrote
A poem who wasn't asked to quote
The choice of all his poetry
Solely from his memory.

Land of Silent Sleep

On Decoration Day both you and I
Will walk once more this wooded path to be
Upon the hill under Kentucky sky
And out the ridge where grows the locust tree,
Where sleep forefathers of this river town
That knows the shadows of this silent hill
Here where our people sleep in hallowed ground
Where it was their destiny to fulfill.
We'll stand once more along the point that shows
The land below that was their yesterday,
The foothills and where Sandy water flows,
The schoolhouse, memories of childhood play,
Where love began and here where it will keep
Forever in this land of silent sleep.

Just Wanted To

Why do we have to have a reason for
Everything in life we choose to do,
A justifiable account for less or more,
What ever happened to *just wanted to*.

Why match intrinsic values one can trace
Down to their most calculable worth
Against esthetic ones you cannot place
Measurable limits on but free at birth.

Why not a life where we alone can choose
Everything without a need to say,
Immeasurable ones stopping to smell a rose,
Calculable ones giving Caesar, Caesar's pay.

Values and reason we alone impose
Where in the end all bills becoming due
Require no justifications for these or those
Other than because *just wanted to*.

Awaiting a Promise Given

And in the end will markers of sandstone
Be hidden by sawbriars and sassafras,
This burial land forsaken and alone,
Forgotten now where only seasons pass.
And will there be no kin to carve again
Their names and epitaphs where now they lay
Illegible by time, by wind, by rain
But once tear-carved and promised there to stay.
And will it be as some who grieved had said
That time would be the healer of all things
Including death and epitaphs that read
Of names and love and of eternal spring.
Unmarked graves left in a sawbriared land
Of those who sleep awaiting a promise planned.

Catlettsburg

A half a mile wide and three miles long
Of land that makes a town,
That hums a foothill-river song
And memories abound,
Buildings made from home-kilned brick,
Mortar home-river sand,
One main street that cuts its niche
The center of the town,
A grocery, hardware, clothing store,
A flag atop a pole,
A gargoyle since days of yore
Hovering the picture show,
The school, schoolyard where once we played—
All things that grew to be,
In spite of efforts to delay
An aged memory.

To Sprout Again

And now I stand upon this rugged slope
Age-scarred and wrinkled as red mountain clay,
Gambling for time, pretending that all hope
To sprout again is now for quick decay;
Brittle-backed I can no longer bend
To scratch this younger dream here in the dust,
Nor can I sing of youth to mountain winds,
Time-sapped youth lies beneath sun-hardened crust.
I'll stand content, that is until this cloud
Hovered so low the naked eye can see
Is harrowed by the bony ridge and plowed
To furrows that might grow eternity:
Aching to stretch, I'll poke into white loam,
Dreaming to sprout new roots in land of home.

To Run a Trotline

Here where the waters flow two rivers wide
I search to find a snag, conceal and tie
My trotline making sure at high/low tide
To leave no giveaway to passersby,
Not knowing their intent or travel to
By johnboat up or down as current flows
Fish-wise to steal or pleasure-passing through
I leave no trace for either one to know.
I stretch my trotline, one hundred niblines long
And bait with doughballs boiled in water that
I've scented with Sweet Anise until strong
Enough to coax and catch the Channel Cats.
A way of life, summers of youth begun
Upon two rivers, a trot to bait and run.

Night Moth

She came that night but did not stay
Because she had but one more day
Of three to live, to fly aloft
In which to show her beauty off.

The Ballad of Grandpa Clark

Up before the children woke
He left before the daylight broke
To mine for coal by carbide light
Where touch was often used for sight.

There was no rain, there was no sun
Deep in the mine, no time begun
Where day was night and night was day
The cost a life for miners' pay.

A pay spent at the company store
With need always a penny more
Where earning was by blood and sweat
And certain was a miner's debt.

And once I heard my grandma say
That Grandpa picked his life away;
On starless nights the cold wind moans
The misery of the miners' bones.

And on the nights the wind was still
Her sadness marked by whippoorwill
I watched her waiting in the dark
Her years away for Grandpa Clark.

Mountain Love

A mountain boy,
An old pin oak,
A Barlow knife,
A careful stroke,
Falling chips,
A blushing grin:
—I love you!
Engraved within.

Strip Mining

There was a ridge I used to know
Along which men discovered coal
And choosing to commercialize
Bulldozed it bare beneath the sky
Deep down where nothing then would grow.

With promise they would plant it new
Gouged deep and sunlight fell onto
Human bones no one to know
Buried there so long ago
Unmarked and left now to undo.

Barren clay, decaying bones,
A gutted land of roots and stones
Left with scars that never heal
And scattered bones that now fill
Open graves no one bemoans.

Stripped of coal and keepers of
Those who claimed environmental love,
Desecrated bones and seed
Bulldozed in mounds of waste and greed
Strip mined of everything thereof

And will it be as ages roll
That my bones will lie with coal,
Mixed with roots and leaves and mold
That coax men as in days of old
Who care not for the human soul.

And if thus should be my plight
Truth is, the end should serve me right
For I once watched a mountain die
Made no protest, gave no cry
And willed a scar eternal sight.

The Gift of Catlettscreek

Upon viewing the creek from the Levi Hampton House

If I could give to you it would not be
Of monetary worth as values go,
Rather, a gift of saved-up memories
Found along a creek so long ago;
A birdsong land where stonecrop and stichwort grew
With crested iris and creeping bugleweed,
Wild sweet williams near water pure as dew
Sand-filtered clear fulfilling any need
To drink, to swim, to fish—whichever choice,
A place to slip away day-on-day's-end
From outside world and sound of human voice
Or designated start or time to spend.
A passed-on memory of which I speak
Once found along the banks of Catlettscreek.

Riverplay

Once upon a river's shore
I saw a white-barked sycamore
With spreading limbs and reddish balls
On puppet strings like dancing dolls—
A play of tree and river blend,
The puppeteer the sightless wind.
And under spider-legged roots
A frog had made a bed that suits,
Reserved mudseat to watch the play
From safety of his hideaway.
And I with nothing planned to do,
Enthralled, I took the play in, too,
Chose a seat beneath the tree
And watched the magic puppetry.

Snowflakes

No two snowflakes are alike
Or so the scientists say
Who dabble in such poppycock
As if to make their day,

But falling from a laden sky
They look the same to me
As they must have in days of old
Just white and Christmassy,

Still a young child's wanted gift,
On Christmas Eve his prayer,
Snowflakes are made for Christmas Day
Without reason to compare.

Return of the Snowbirds

I have waited a summer's/autumn's time to see
Snowbirds return to eat pecans and be
Home again in my backyard and free
To sing and sit there, in the pecan tree.

Their helter-skelter pace is without sound
Tiptoeing the trunk headfirst and then headdown
Wherever oval hull-shucked nuts are found
Squirrel-cracked or Bluejay-dropped to ground.

Or from an unidentifiable source to pay
A donor's gift in hopes to silent say
That he has window-watched the time away
For their return home for a winter's stay.

The Great Horned Owl

Once I saw a Great Horned Owl
At dusk in Black Oak tree,
Both beauty and his deadliness
Marked his symmetry,

This nighttime tiger of the wood,
Fearless, seemed not to know
Though acute of ear and keen of sight
I watched him from below.

I saw him drop from leafless limbs,
Hang silent in midair
If not silhouetted against the sky
I would not have seen him there,

Or learned that day that opposites
Like beauty is to death
Could coexist within one heart,
Strike in a single breath.

Nightriver

Far up the river on the darkest night
To run a trotline tied to a willow tree,
A long way home downriver without a light,
A rising fog now hides the shore from me.
With pull of oars the oarlock's screeching sound
Breaks the river's silence and I throw
Water on locks to quiet then search for ground,
Tieing-off to await the moon before I go.
A light from moon in silver maples there
Along both banks their tops above the fog,
A moonbeam path is made and with great care
I thread the boat through brush and drifting log.
Between illuminated maple trees that show
My way downriver as I homeward row.

Legend of the Writing Spider

(To Ruth—this to you in verse)
Big Sandy legend saying if the black and yellow
Writing Spider (Corn Spider) hears your name and
writes it across his web, you will shrivel up and die before
the sun goes down.

You are a pretty spider but
I am afraid of you,
Your home web-spun on shocks of corn
Luminous with morning dew,
Drip, dripping on the stubble below
In mesmerizing tone
While you watch with omen eyes
From your inverted cone
Of whirling darkness, mystic, deep,
Your place to plot at night
To coax the name from who day-pass
Your pencil-legs to write
In zigzag strands of wider stroke
The name of whom you found
To cast your spell and shrivel-up before
The sun goes down.
Black and yellow Writing Spider
I fear with coming day
Someone will see me shucking corn
And give my name away.

A Note on Feeding Winter Birds

I'm out to winter-feed the birds
For songs made in the spring,
For summer melodies I've heard
That didn't cost a thing,
I'll brush a clearing in the snow
Where they can find the ground
And while tree-watched pretend not-know
Then sprinkle feed around.

Inconspicuous, with time to spare
I'll stay a winter song,
If you return before I'm there,
Wait—I won't be long.

How the Recall Goes

For I have lived my life from deep within
These timeless hills, and often I recall
The moon among the trees, its slow ascent
Above a bony ridge a cloud-touch tall;
Time of rebirth upon spring-budding trees,
Then summer-aged, leaf-dressed in autumn hue,
The hills laced with hoar frost spun delicately
To memory-keep where sun cannot undo;
A time of snow and ice, of freezing cold,
Sounds of splitting ax and crosscut saw,
Of promise made, a promise ages old,
Saying this too will pass come winter's thaw.
For I have lived my life, have come to know
Often life is how the recall goes.

Decoration Day on the River

I watch them at the river throw
Out wreaths of flowers in memory
Of kin in hopes as currents go
They float over the watery
Place only the river knows
Among the snags or dropoff holes
Of unmarked graves of last repose.

Silent, the river does not say,
No epitaph along the shore
Of where or how that fateful day
They lost their lives for evermore,
By summer swim or foolish play,
By their own hand or other way,
The timeless river will not say.

I watch the wreaths slow-wind their way
Downriver on Decoration Day.

Zacchaeus

They say:
Zacchaeus in days of yore
climbed up in a sycamore
High enough the Lord to see
And gave a touch of history
For what was until a common tree.

I say:
Of what they say I'm not quite sure
That's as regards the sycamore,
It could have been for us to see
Purpose in commonality
And dignity, not history.

The Leaning Tower

Often I dwell where a house once stood
That leaned by the mouth of Catlettscreek
Built on a narrow, sandy streak
Of riverland, and flood-made weak,
A dwelling made of clapboard wood.

Buckled boards that played wind songs,
A house town-named The Leaning Tower,
Predictions told the day, the hour
A coming flood would overpower—
A life that time could not prolong.

Two stories tall as dwellings go,
Up crow's foot high I scanned the land,
Listened for sounds from river's bend
Of paddle wheels with tows of sand
Or tows heaped with Big Sandy coal.

Here where the creek and river met
I whiled the summer days away
Fishing, sand-writing dreams to say
That one day I would slip away

And be a river pilot yet.
Where in a winter world I'd go
Ofttimes to river's edge to see
Snowflakes wind-dancing through the trees
And patterns woven delicately
By winter's touch on ice and snow.

Here where now a floodwall stands,
This place where once upon a year
A boy and Leaning Tower were here
When river was their overseer,
And left no trace upon the land.

I Will Not Grieve Again

I will not grieve again that day I step
Upon Kentucky land that knows my birth,
Then bend to whisper of a promise kept
Of my return here to this sacred earth;
A place of riversong and cawing crow,
Of whippoorwill and haunting call of dove,
A land akin to rain, to sun, to snow,
Log home with trailing chimney smoke above;
Mule-made clearing planted to eight-row corn
That's scarecrow kept, tended by a child
Garden-framed by briars and needle thorn,
Grubbing the clearing back inside the wild.
Land of my childhood, scenes of memory,
To step, to bend, to hear, whisper, to be.

I Stayed to Watch
a Water Spider Once

To Tina Dean

I watched a water spider once
Weaving herself a sail
Inside a cove of grass and reeds
Beside a brown cattail,
I saw the tiny, silken threads
Glinting from the sun,
Then stayed to see the work complete
And with her rigging done,
I saw her scull outside the cove
Remembering how that day
It was the wind that caught her sail
And carried her away.

The Gypsies' Curse

To Dr. Alfonso Lombana,
my great friend who also knew the Gypsies

The Gypsies used to come each spring
To Ice Dam Creek to dance and sing
And when the day turned into night
Circling inside their driftwood light
We heard ghost stories centuries old
While Mommy had her fortune told,
Greasing the teller's palm while we
Heard the moaning willow trees
Intermixed with words to scare
With wind-combed strands of witches hair;
And back around the mountainside
We tucked in close in hopes to hide
And dodge brush-bones along the path
Escaping vengeful witches' wrath.
And Mommy dodging nothing swore
That what was said she'd heard before,
Palm-lines upon her hands foretold
Of nothing new, of nothing old
Which all in all made matters worse:
Cross a Gypsy, bring a curse.
She swore she'd never traipse again
Where foretelling was a sin.
And yet it was not Mommy's say
That sent the Gypsies on their way:
One spring they simply did not show
Left nothing here for us to know
Except for better or for worse
A longing—call it Gypsies' curse.